Make in a Day
CRAFTS FOR KIDS

Cintia Gonzalez-Pell

Dover Publications, Inc.
Mineola, New York

Bibliographical Note

Make in a Day: Crafts for Kids is a new work,
first published by Dover Publications, Inc., in 2017.

Library of Congress Cataloging-in-Publication Data

Names: Gonzalez-Pell, Cintia, author.
Title: Make in a day : crafts for kids / Cintia Gonzalez-Pell.
Description: Mineola, New York : Dover Publications, Inc., [2017] | Audience:
    Age: 7–12.
Identifiers: LCCN 2017028149| ISBN 9780486813738 | ISBN 0486813738
Subjects: LCSH: Handicraft—Juvenile literature.
Classification: LCC TT160 .G64 2018 | DDC 745.5—dc23
LC record available at https://lccn.loc.gov/2017028149

Manufactured in the United States by LSC Communications
81373801   2017
www.doverpublications.com

CONTENTS

I was always a crafty kid growing up. My mum taught me to sew by letting me help her when she was making clothes for my sister and me. I would help her trace the patterns and pin the fabric. Later she taught me to crochet and stitch, and I would always be working on one crafty project or another to keep me entertained. I would even take my crochet to school and work on it during recess sometimes! My favorite class at school was art, and I was lucky enough to have several teachers who always encouraged my creativity.

After many years following a professional career as a pharmacist, I rediscovered my love of crafting and the *My Poppet* blog was born. On *mypoppet.com.au* I share craft projects with step-by-step instructions with readers from all over the world. I've designed and made hundreds of craft projects for my blog, craft books, and magazines, and the one thing they all have in common is that they are colorful and fun to make.

Now that I'm a mum myself, I enjoy crafting with my own daughter, Emma, who is 8. She has reminded me of how capable and creative kids can be. All of the projects in this book are inspired by activities Emma and I have made together, or things that I enjoyed making as a kid.

A special note for kids reading this: I encourage you to use these ideas as a guide and just have fun! Don't worry if your own craft projects don't look exactly like the ones in the pictures. Injecting your own personal style will make your projects extra special.

Make one project or make them all! Why not make a few as gifts for special friends or family members?

Enjoy crafting!
Cintia Gonzalez-Pell

Artistic Abstract Painted Canvas

You don't have to be a Picasso or van Gogh to create your own unique piece of art to decorate your walls. This abstract canvas art is easy to make and will unleash your hidden artist! Have fun discovering how your favorite colors blend together. (Younger children may enjoy painting with their fingers instead of brushes.)

To make this project, you will need:

* Stretched canvas

* Acrylic paint in assorted colors

* Acrylic paint in white

* Removable adhesive dots or stickers

* Painter's masking tape

* Paintbrushes

* Jar and water

* Plastic tablecloth or newspaper to protect surfaces

1 Dab small blobs of paint onto your canvas.

2 With a slightly damp paintbrush, blend the colors together. Leave alone to dry well.

3 Stick a design onto your canvas with masking tape and/or stickers. Press the edges of the tape down firmly to prevent paint from bleeding underneath.

4 Paint the entire canvas with white paint and allow to dry thoroughly. If the white paint doesn't cover well with one coat, leave to dry and add a second coat.

5 Carefully peel off your tape and stickers to reveal your art. You can touch up spots if you find your paint has bled under the taped sections.

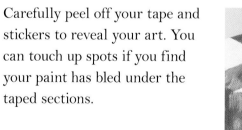

Painted Animal Gift Box

Instead of wrapping your next gift in paper that just gets thrown away, why not make an adorable animal gift box? I can guarantee the giftee will enjoy the packaging just as much as the treats inside. Make a whole menagerie for yourself; these little boxes are fantastic for storing bits and pieces such as small toys, hair clips, and craft supplies.

* Round cardboard gift box with lid

* Acrylic paint

* Paintbrushes

* Pencil

* Googly eyes

* Glue

* Craft felt and/or pompoms

* Paint dish

* Jar and water

* Plastic tablecloth or newspaper to protect surfaces

1 Sketch out your animal face design on the lid of your gift box. Be creative; animals with stripes and spots are lots of fun.

2 Paint the main color of your design on the lid and set aside to dry.

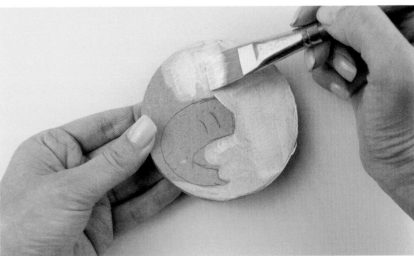

3 Paint the outside of the gift box base and set aside to dry. If your animal has a patterned body, add some of the pattern to the outside of your gift box.

4 Paint onto the lid the details of the animal's facial features such as a nose, whiskers, and rosy cheeks. Leave to dry.

5 Cut out ear shapes from the felt. You can also use pompoms for the ears if you'd like.

6 Glue on ears.

7 Glue on googly eyes.

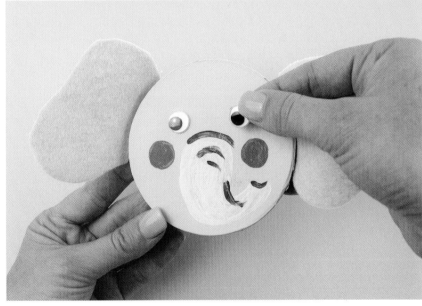

8 Now your gift box is ready to fill with goodies.

Personalized Sneakers

Turn your boring canvas sneakers into a real fashion statement. Add just a subtle pattern or go all out and create something eye-popping. Your left and right shoes don't even have to match! Let your design reflect your personality or the things you like the most. If you are stuck for ideas, try including the colors of your favorite sports team, or get inspired by a cartoon or movie character you enjoy.

To make this project, you will need:

* White canvas sneakers

* Pencil

* Permanent markers of various colors

* Black permanent marker (optional)

* Plastic tablecloth or newspaper to protect surfaces

 Remove the shoelaces from your sneakers and set aside.

 With a pencil lightly draw your design onto the sneakers. It's up to you if you want your right and left sneaker to match each other, or if you will have a unique design for each one.

 Trace your design with the colored markers, starting with the tongue of each sneaker. This is an inconspicuous place to test your colors.

4 Working on one section of your sneakers at a time, continue to color in your design with the markers.

5 Once you have added all of the colored patterns to your sneakers, outline your design with a black marker if desired.

6 Replace the laces on your sneakers. Now they are ready to wear!

Recycled Sweater Gadget Cozy

NOTE: Adult supervision or help required

Keep your music player, electronic game, phone, or tablet safe and sound in its own custom-made gadget cozy. Made from an old sweater, this project is a great way to upcycle a garment that may have gone to the trash heap. No fancy sewing skills are required; just a basic running stitch is all you need to know to quickly whip up this gadget cover. If you don't have any old sweaters handy, store-bought felt works just as well.

To make this project, you will need:

* Electronic gadget
* Old sweater or craft felt
* Embroidery floss
* Embroidery needle

* Button
* Sharp scissors
* Pins
* Marker

1 Before you cut into any clothing, check with an adult to make sure it's okay. Find an old woolen sweater that has been accidentally shrunk (felted) in the wash, or throw an old sweater in a hot wash cycle to felt it on purpose.

2 Fold the sweater in half and place your gadget near the bottom edge. With the marker, draw an outline around your device about ½" wider than the gadget.

3 Pin the two layers together and cut on the marked line.

4 Thread your needle with embroidery floss and tie a knot at the end.

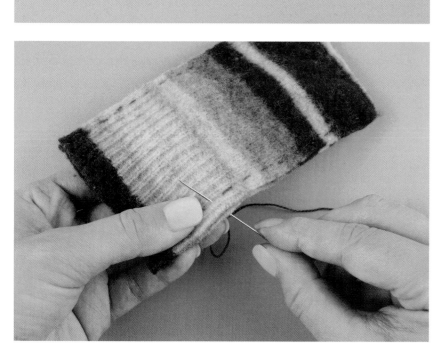

5 Leaving a border of about ¼" from the edge, sew the two layers together with a running stitch. To do a running stitch, simply bring the needle over and under, catching both layers of fabric. Make sure you leave the top open. Tie a knot in the thread at the end to finish, and cut excess thread.

Cut a 1¼" x 4" rectangle shape from the leftover sweater fabric to make a tab. Cut a small slit in one end just large enough to fit your button through.

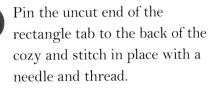 Pin the uncut end of the rectangle tab to the back of the cozy and stitch in place with a needle and thread.

8 Fold the tab over to the front and mark where the button needs to go. Sew on your button, and your sweater gadget cozy is ready!

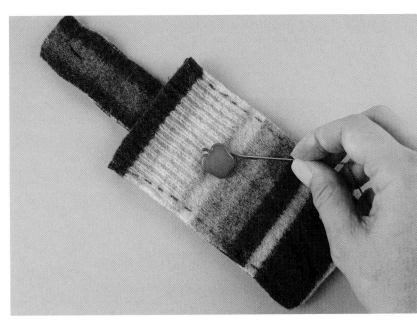

Colorful Yarn Dreamcatcher

A dreamcatcher is a whimsical way to add a pop of color to your bedroom, with the added bonus that it will catch all of your sweet dreams before they fly out the window! This project is perfect for using up some of those scraps of yarn and trims that have been languishing at the bottom of your family's craft basket. Go ahead and add feathers, beads, and even pompoms for extra decoration.

To make this project, you will need:

* Embroidery hoop

* Thin craft cords or assorted yarns

* Ribbons

* Wooden beads

* Pompom trims or lace

* Feathers

* Yarn needle

* Scissors

1. Separate the outer part of the embroidery hoop from the inner part and set aside the outer part for later.

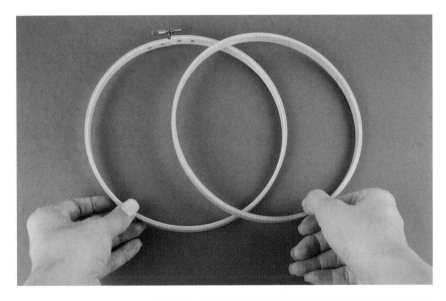

2. Thread some wooden beads onto the thin cord or yarn and then attach the cord to the inner hoop with a small knot. Start to wrap the cord over and around the hoop to create a spiderweb crisscross design. Tie a knot to secure.

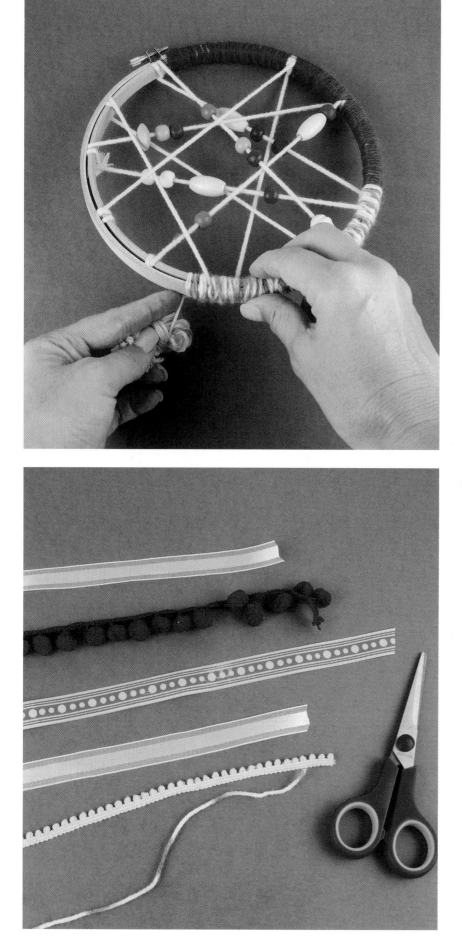

3 Replace the large hoop over the small hoop and tighten the screw if required. Wrap colorful yarn around the edge of both hoops, and secure with a knot to finish.

4 Cut several 15–20" lengths of ribbons, yarns, and trims to be the fringe decorations.

With the metal screw of the
hoop toward the top, tie the
trims and yarns onto the
bottom of the hoop.

 Decorate the fringes by
threading wooden beads onto
the yarn with a needle and
tying on feathers.

Tie a small loop of yarn to
the metal screw. You can add
a bead if you'd like. Now your
dreamcatcher is ready to hang.

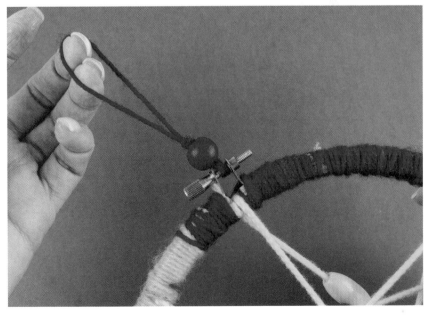

Fuse Bead Bag Charms

NOTE: *Adult supervision or help required*

At my daughter Emma's school, it's super trendy to add lots of key rings and bag charms to your schoolbag or backpack as a way to express your interests. The beauty of fuse beads is that you can make them into practically any design you choose. Why not make matching bag charms for you and your best friend?

To make this project, you will need:

- Fuse beads
- Fuse bead board
- Wax paper
- Iron

- Jewelry pliers
- Key ring clip or lobster clasp
- Large jump rings

1 Create your favorite fuse bead design on the bead board.

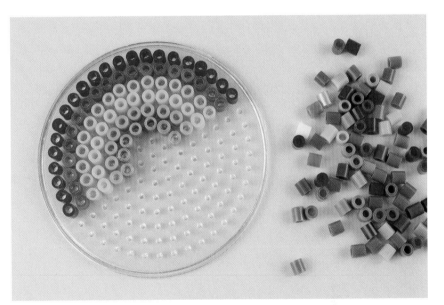

2 When you are happy with your pattern, place a piece of wax paper over the top of it.

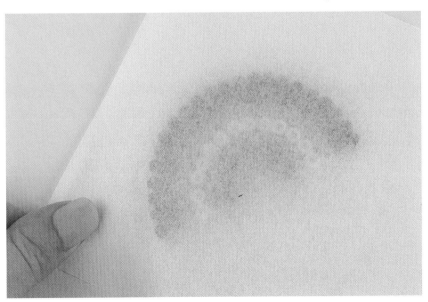

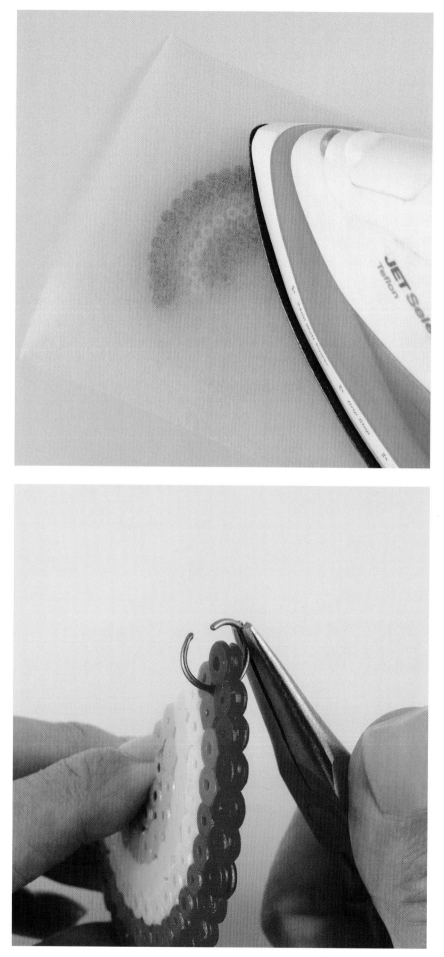

3 Ask an adult to iron your design (using a medium-hot iron with no steam), gently pressing over the bead design until the beads are melted together slightly. Iron both sides.

4 Open the jump ring with pliers and thread the jump ring through one of the holes in the beads.

5 Add the clasp to the jump ring.

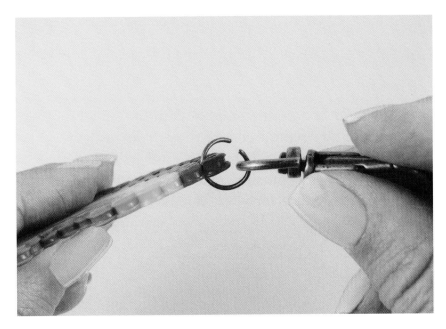

6 Using pliers, close the jump ring to secure.

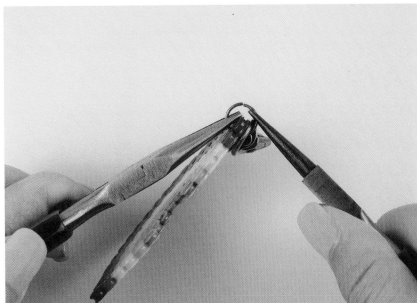

7 If you would like, you can add more than one charm to your key ring clip or lobster clasp.

Felt Pennant Flag

Give your bedroom wall or bulletin board a bit of vintage flair with a cheerful felt pennant flag reminiscent of those from yesteryear. Personalize it with your name, that of your favorite team, or a catchy slogan. If you are feeling extra creative, add some more felt embellishments such as flowers or stars. These flags make great birthday presents for your friends!

To make this project, you will need:

* Large sheets of craft felt in two contrasting colors

* Smaller sheet of craft felt in a third color (shown here in gray)

* Ruler

* Pencil or marker

* Piece of paper (optional)

* Scissors

* Craft glue

* Pins

* Heavy book

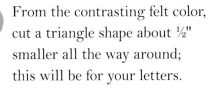

1 From the main flag color, cut a long triangle shape measuring 11" long with a base of 7" wide.

2 From the contrasting felt color, cut a triangle shape about ½" smaller all the way around; this will be for your letters.

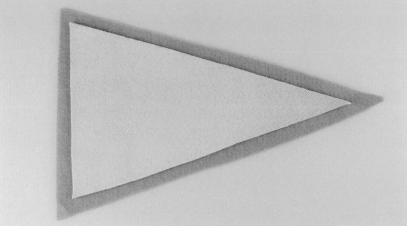

3 Count how many letters you need for the name and mark matching sections on the smaller triangle of felt.

4 Cut out the letters of the name carefully. If you are not confident cutting out letters directly from the felt, sketch them on a piece of paper, then use the paper letters as a template.

5 Arrange your letters on the large felt triangle. Add small dabs of glue to the back of the letters, one at a time, and glue them back into place.

6 From the gray felt, cut one narrow 7" strip and two narrow 5" strips. Fold the small strips in half to form a V shape and pin to the short side of the flag.

7 Top with the long strip of gray felt and glue into place at the base of the flag (short side). Don't forget to remove the pins.

8 Weigh down with a heavy book and leave to dry.

Fruity Plant Pots

Start your own potted garden in these fun and fruity plant pots. Line them up on a sunny window ledge filled with herbs or easy-to-grow succulents. Don't have a green thumb? Don't worry, these fruity plant pots are also the perfect desk organizers to keep your supply of pens, pencils, and markers. Paint markers are quick drying, which makes it easy to add details to the pots, such as the seeds. Strawberry, Pineapple, or Watermelon—which one do you like the most?

To make this project, you will need:

* Small terra-cotta plant pots
* Pencil
* Ceramic and terra-cotta markers or paint markers in red, pink, black, white, green, and yellow
* Potting mix and plants
* Plastic tablecloth or newspaper to protect surfaces

1 Sketch your design onto the pot. The pineapple pot will have zigzag patterns; the strawberry pot will have a scalloped border on top with seeds; and the watermelon pot will have stripes at the top and seeds. Use the finished picture as a guide.

2 Paint in the design for the pineapple pot completely in yellow.

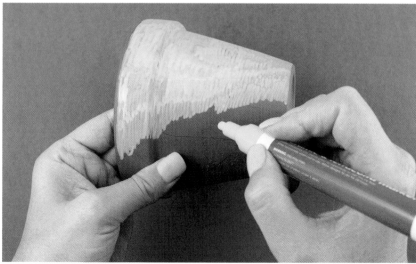

Let the yellow marker dry and then add the zigzag shapes in black.

 For the strawberry pot, paint the leaf area green and the body in red. Leave to dry.

 Add the strawberry seeds in yellow.

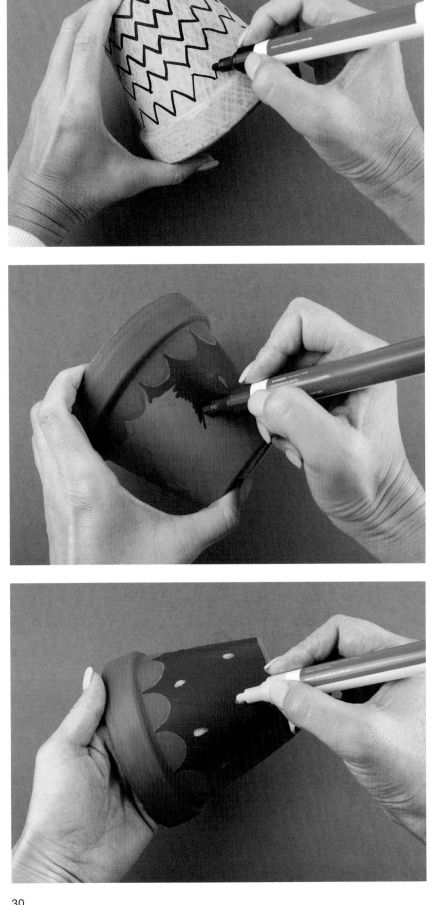

To make the watermelon pot, paint a green stripe on the top rim, then a narrow white stripe, finishing with pink for the rest of the body. Leave to dry.

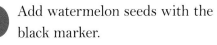 Add watermelon seeds with the black marker.

 When all your pots are fully dry, you can add your plants.

Drawstring Treasure Pouch

Where do you keep your treasures? Pirates, knights, and medieval maidens held their valuables in leather pouches just like these, and now you can too. Feel free to make your pouch as small or as large as you'd like so it will keep all your special treasures safe. Faux leather or felt will work just as well as leather.

To make this project, you will need:

* Plate
* Leather or faux leather larger than the plate
* Marker
* Scissors

* Hole puncher
* Suede lashing or cord
* Wooden bead with large hole
* Assorted decorative beads

 1 Place the plate on the back of your leather and with a marker trace around the edge to make a circle shape. For a big pouch, use a dinner plate; for a smaller pouch, a side plate will do.

2 Cut out your circle shape with scissors.

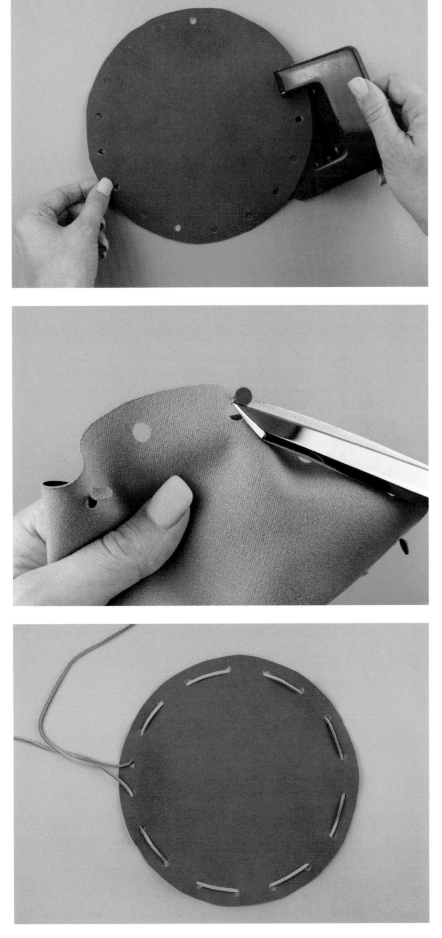

3. Using a hole puncher, punch holes about 1" apart all the way around the edge of the circle.

4. If needed, trim off any little circles that are still hanging on to the leather.

5. Thread your cord in and out through the holes, making sure the cord starts and finishes on the side of the leather you want to show on the outside of your pouch. If you have an odd number of holes, your cord will start and finish in the same hole. If you have an even amount of holes, the cords will start and finish in holes next to each other.

6 Pull the cord to cinch the pouch halfway, and thread both cord ends through a large bead.

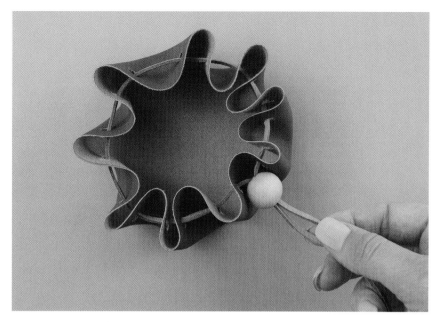

7 Add decorative beads to the cords, then tie small knots on the end of each cord to secure the beads. Trim off excess cord.

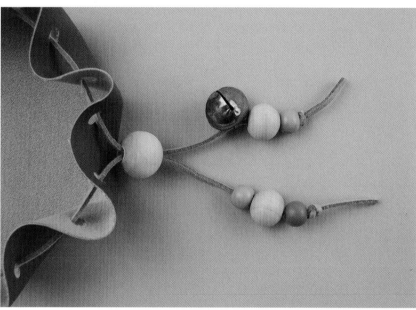

8 Fill your pouch with treasures, and then push the wooden bead down to close the pouch completely.

Paper Plate Doughnut Garland

When Emma was little she was so obsessed with doughnuts that she requested a doughnut-themed party for her third birthday. We crafted this garland while the cake was baking, and it made the perfect party décor. Afterwards it hung in her room for a long time because it was just so dang cute. A great party project, each guest can make their own doughnut to take home or to combine and string up as a garland. Don't like pink frosting? Use brown paper and make a chocolate-glazed doughnut instead.

To make this project, you will need:

* Paper plates
* Pink craft paper
* Confetti
* Glue stick

* Scissors
* Hole punch
* Yarn or string

1 Flatten out as many paper plates as you need for your garland, and draw a small circle in the center of each.

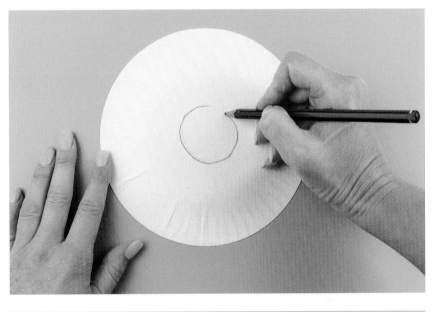

2 Cut out a hole in the center of each of your plates.

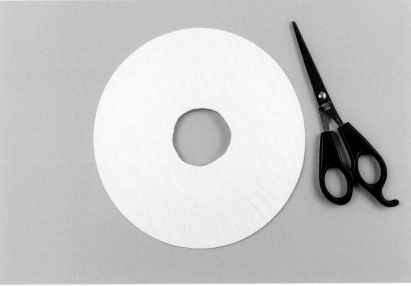

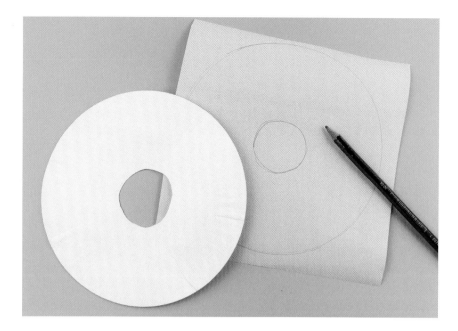

3 Using one of the paper plates as a template, draw ring shapes onto your pink paper. The pink paper will be the doughnut frosting.

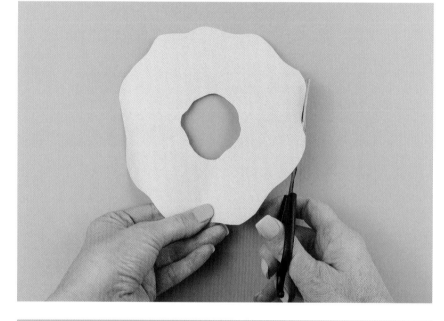

4 Cut out the pink paper frosting a little smaller than the tracing lines, making wobbly edges.

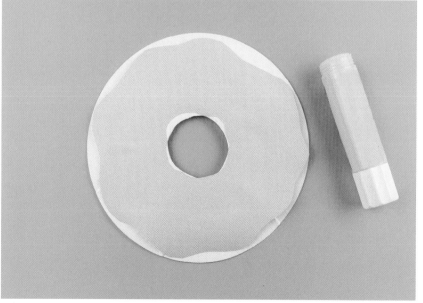

5 Stick your pink frosting paper onto your paper plate with a glue stick.

6 Use the glue stick to cover half of the pink frosting paper, then stick on the confetti to look like sprinkles.

7 With a hole puncher, punch two holes near the top of all the paper plates.

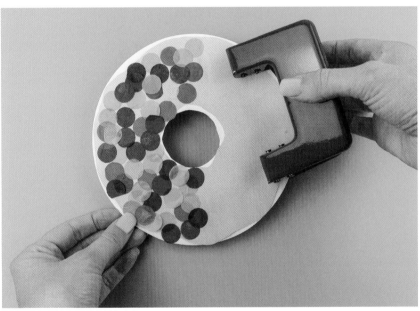

8 Thread the paper doughnuts onto your yarn or string. Tie loops at both ends. Now your doughnut garland is ready to hang.

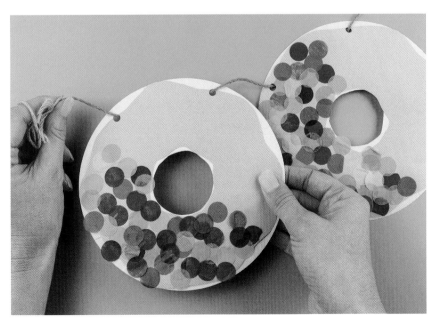

Decorated Wooden Bangles

Bangles are a fun way to accessorize any outfit. Here I am showing you three unique ways to transform a plain wooden bangle into something a little bit fancy. These make great gifts for Mother's Day or as a special gift for your favorite friend or teacher. Get together with a group of friends and make a bunch of bangles to sell at a fund-raising fair.

To make this project, you will need:

* Wooden bangles
* PVA glue (white glue)
* Masking tape
* Assorted acrylic paints, including white
* Paper confetti or tissue paper
* Washi tape

* Scissors
* Paintbrushes
* Paint dishes
* Jar and water
* Plastic tablecloth or newspaper to protect surfaces
* Chopstick and two glasses for a drying stand

1. For the washi tape-covered bangle, choose your favorite tape designs and cut strips long enough to wrap all the way around the outside and inside of the bangle. Stick the tape on firmly.

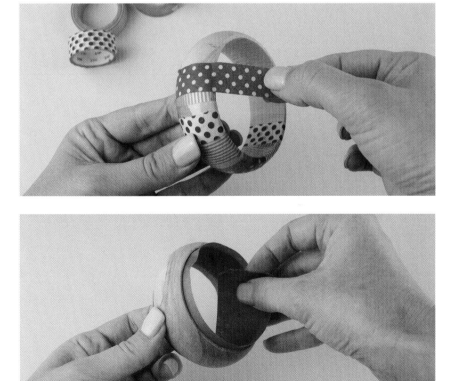

2. For the painted bangle, tape the inside of the bangle with masking tape to keep the inside surface clean.

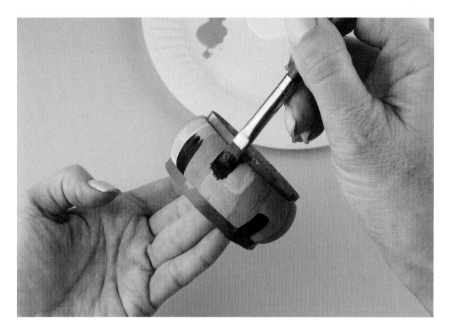

 Choose your favorite paint colors and paint on a design. You can paint spots, stripes, or even flowers. Be creative!

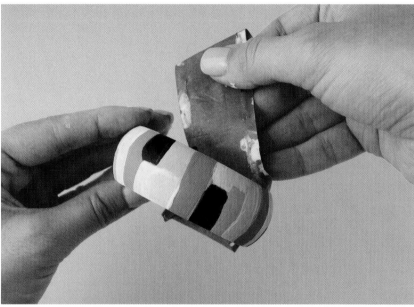

4 Allow the paint to dry, and then remove the masking tape.

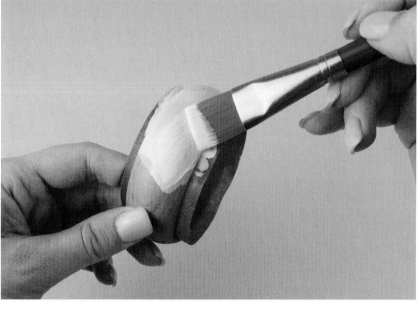

5 For the decoupage bangle, tape the inside of the bangle with masking tape to keep the inside surface clean. Paint with a coat of white paint. Leave to dry.

6 Working in small sections at a time, apply a thin coat of PVA glue to the bangle with a separate paintbrush and stick on confetti pieces one at a time. Keep working until the whole outside of the bangle is covered.

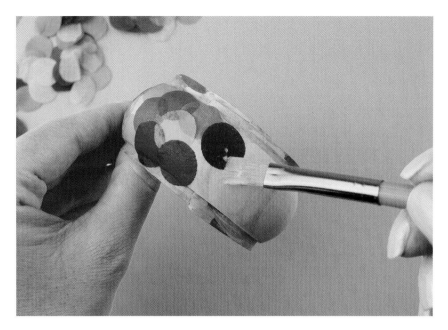

7 Allow to dry and remove the masking tape. Trim off any loose bits of confetti to neaten.

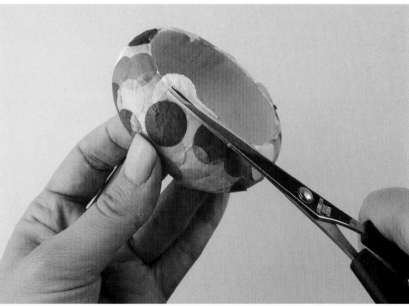

8 Seal each bangle with a couple of layers of watered-down PVA glue inside and out, allowing drying time between each coat. You can use a chopstick balanced on two glasses to make a drying stand.

Multicolored Branch Weaving

Emma is forever bringing home sticks and branches that she finds on our evening walks around the neighborhood. Most of them end up in a little pile in the garden, but occasionally she finds an interesting forked branch that is just perfect for a little bit of weaving. If you've ever tried weaving on a loom, you will find this project a breeze. The organic shape of the branch allows for a more free-form approach. Have fun with this project!

* Y-shaped branch
* Yarn in assorted colors
* Yarn needle

* Wide-tooth comb
* Scissors

1 Find a Y-shaped branch; you'll be working in the V-shaped section of it.

2 Tie some yarn onto the bottom of the V shape on your branch.

45

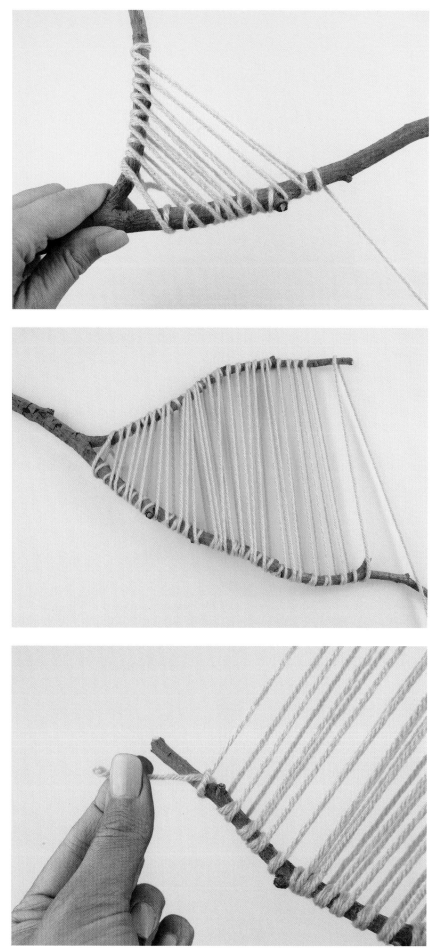

3 Start winding the yarn around and across the V shape firmly so it doesn't slip.

4 Continue to work all the way up the branch arms. This section is called the *warp*.

5 Tie a knot at the top to secure. Trim off excess yarn.

6 To start the weaving, tie on your first color and thread a yarn needle with about one yard (36") of yarn.

7 With your needle, weave the yarn in front of and then behind the warp threads until you get to the end. On the way back do the same, but this time in the opposite pattern; where your yarn went in front in the previous row, it will now go behind.

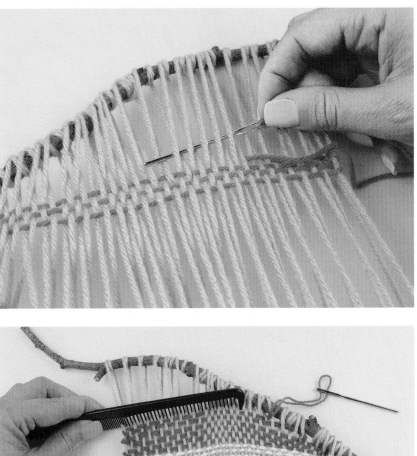

8 Change colors as you go to make interesting patterns. Use the comb to press down on the weaving and make it even. Continue until your V shape is full, then tie a knot at the end to secure. Weave in any loose yarn tails.

Paper Napkin Papier Mâché Dish

Keep your trinkets, small toys, hair accessories, and jewelry tidy in these colorful papier mâché dishes. Perfect for keeping small stuff contained, they are not only practical but fun to make too. You probably have all of the supplies you need for this project already, so you can get started right away. Any plain paper napkins are suitable for this project, but printed napkins with bold graphic designs really add extra personality to your dish.

To make this project, you will need:

* Plain or printed paper napkins
* PVA glue (white glue)
* Glass jar with lid
* Small metal or ceramic bowl
* Plastic wrap
* Paintbrush
* Water
* Scissors
* Hair dryer (optional)

1 Choose a small metal or ceramic bowl as a mold and cover the outside with plastic wrap.

2 Make your glue mixture by adding two parts glue to one part water in a glass jar. Close the lid and shake well to combine.

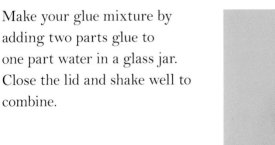

3 Separate the layers of each paper napkin. Each layer is called a *ply*. Most napkins are 2–3 ply, and printed napkins usually have two white layers and one printed layer. Set aside the printed layers.

4 Rip up the white napkin layers into strips.

5 Coat the plastic wrap over the mold with glue mixture using a paintbrush, and lay the strips of white napkin over in a crisscross pattern to cover the whole mold.

6 Continue adding layers of paper and glue, drying between layers with a hair dryer if you want to speed up the process. The more layers you add, the stronger your bowl will be. I suggest 10–20 layers. Leave to dry fully.

7 Once dry, remove the bowl and plastic wrap. Glue on a layer of printed napkin to the inside of the dish, finishing with an extra coat of glue, and leave to dry.

8 Trim off the edges with scissors to neaten.

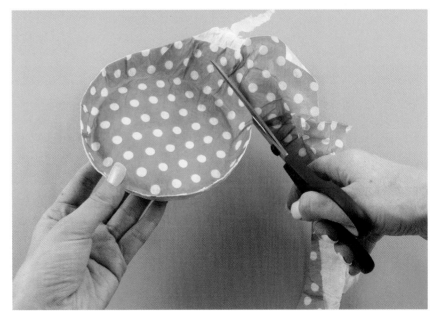

Paint Your Own Pillowcase

NOTE: Adult supervision or help required

It's easy to create your own custom-designed bedding with just some fabric paint and a little bit of imagination. All you need is a plain pillowcase. Your design can be as simple or as fancy as you would like; techniques such as stamping and stenciling work great for this project too!

To make this project, you will need:

* White cotton pillowcase

* Pencil or tailor's chalk

* Fabric paint

* Paintbrushes

* Paint dish

* Jar and water

* Cardboard rectangle (pillowcase size)

* Plastic tablecloth or newspaper to protect surfaces

* Pressing cloth

* Iron

1 Prewash and iron your pillowcase. Ask an adult to help.

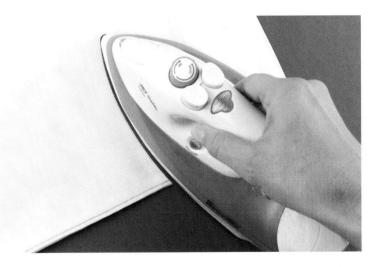

2 Insert a cardboard rectangle into the pillowcase; this will prevent paint from bleeding through the fabric onto the other side.

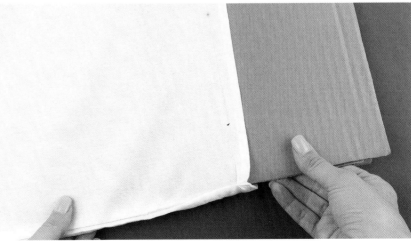

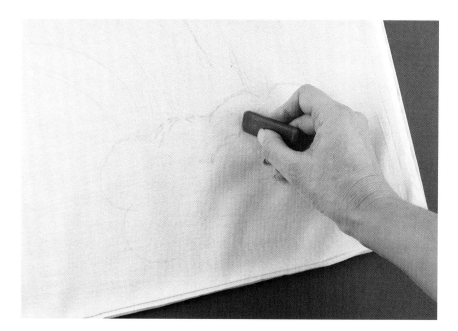

3 Lightly sketch your design onto the pillowcase with a pencil or tailor's chalk.

 4 You may need to mix some paint colors together to get the exact shades you need for your design.

5 Paint on your design, cleaning your brush well between colors. Some colors may need a couple of coats.

6 Allow fabric paint to dry fully. Check the paint manufacturer's instructions as a guide. When completely dry, remove the cardboard insert.

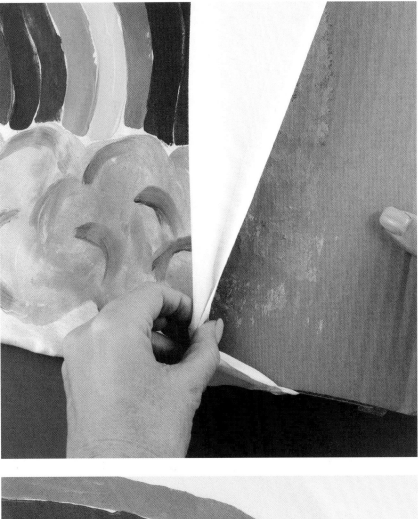

7 If your fabric paint requires a heat setting, ask an adult to iron your design for you. It's best to use a pressing cloth to ensure that the paint doesn't stick to the iron or smudge your design. You may need to wash the pillowcase a couple of times before use to soften the paint.

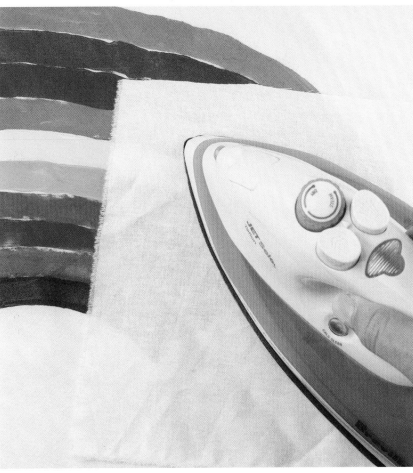

Polymer Clay Bead Necklace and Key Ring

NOTE: Adult supervision or help required

When I was a girl, polymer clay was all the rage. I'd make little sculptures and jewelry out of it. Now that it has had a resurgence in popularity, Emma and I have revisited this versatile material to make a variety of pretty beads that look great strung together to make a necklace or key ring. Polymer clay beads are super easy to make, and it's fun getting creative with lots of different designs. Give it a try.

To make this project, you will need:

* Oven-bake polymer clay in assorted colors, including black and white

* Oven to bake the clay

* Skewer tool or toothpick

* Greaseproof baking paper

* Small baking tray

* Waxed cotton cord or leather strapping

* Necklace clasp (optional)

* Key ring clasp

* Scissors

1 Choose your favorite colors of clay and knead each color to soften. This is called *conditioning* the clay.

2 To make a plain round bead design, break off small pieces of clay and roll into a ball in the palm of your hand. This can be used as a base bead in Steps 3 and 4, or to finish (see Step 6).

3 To make a spotted bead design, roll tiny balls of clay in a contrasting color and place the small balls onto the base bead, then roll the ball between your hands to smooth out. To finish, see Step 6.

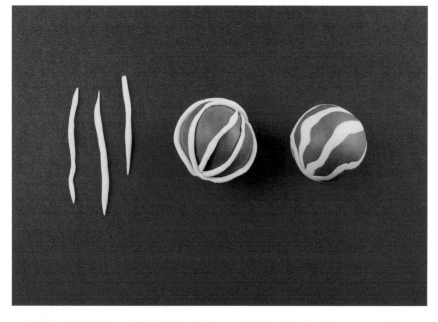

4 To make a striped bead design, roll long, thin ropes in a contrasting color and lay these over the base bead, then roll the ball between your hands to smooth out. To finish, see Step 6.

5 To make a marbled bead design, break off a small amount of black, white, and colored clays and roll them into three long ropes. Twist the rope together and then lightly knead the clay until you get a swirly pattern. Break off small pieces of clay and roll each piece into a ball in the palm of your hand. To finish, see Step 6.

6 Make a hole in your beads with a skewer or toothpick. Make sure the hole is wider than your cord or leather strap.

7 Place all of your beads onto a small baking tray lined with greaseproof baking paper. Ask an adult to help you to bake the beads in an oven following the clay manufacturer's instructions for temperature and timing. Allow to cool fully before the next step.

8 To make a necklace, thread beads onto your waxed cord or leather strapping.

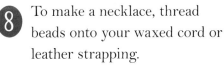

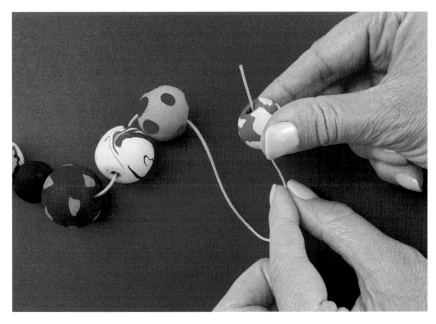

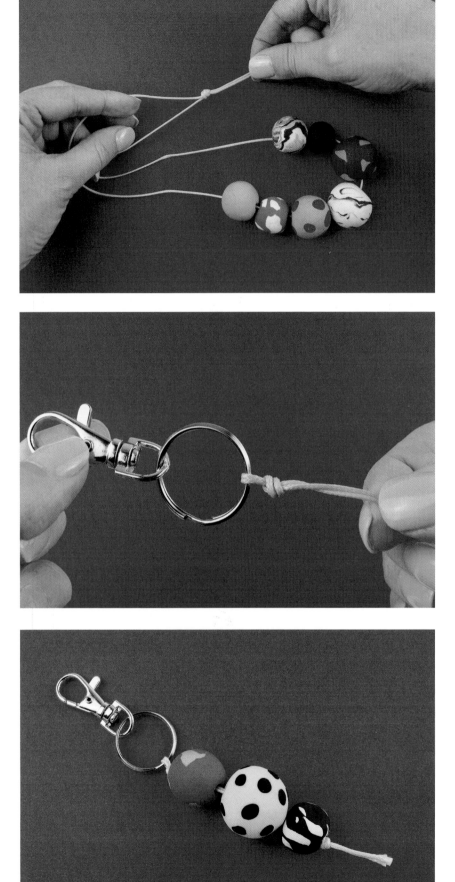

9 Tie off your necklace cord with a knot (or attach a necklace clasp if you prefer). Make sure the necklace is long enough to fit over your head. Trim off excess cord.

10 To make a key ring, fold a 10" piece of cord in half and knot it onto the key ring.

11 Thread both cord tails through three or four beads and secure with a knot on the end. Trim off excess cord.